wish you a happy birthday

You ought to know what a little Fairy told me.

Bonne Année

Bonne Fête

Japon

I'm not acting now.
Est-ce bien vrai, tous ces mensonges?

May all

your days be happy days

If you ever find a tiny flower
With a yellow eye and petals blue
You'll know it's a Fairy-Wishing-flower
And your wishes will all come true.

Die Mädchen sind durch die Bienen,

Sie fliegen ein, sie fliegen aus — Grad wie in einem Bienenhaus,

HEARTY GREETINGS

What is Time to us?

HONESTY

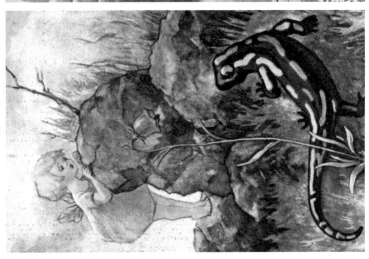

Gattini Francesco = 339. Tribunali = Napoli

Salutations.

She was rather
Grave with George.

ELFINS OF THE BROOK.

SEE HOW THE "SWALLOW-TAIL"
FLUTTERS AND DIPS
NO WONDER THE THIRD FAIRY SLIPS!
LITTLE FAIRY SLIPS!

LARKSPUR

A happy New Year.

DADDYLONGLEGS, FLYING STRONG, PULLS THE MERRY ELVES ALONG: IN AND OUT THEY DART FOR HOURS, THROUGH THE GOLD LABURNUM FLOWERS.

With birthday greetings.

Naught can sever.

Friends forever.

Souvenir Affectueux

CHOSES DE FRANCE
Beautiful Things of France

Arc de Triomphe de l'Étoile

Sept. 29

PARIS-95
15
IX

ME
DE L

Pierre

Clos de

Bou

Lib

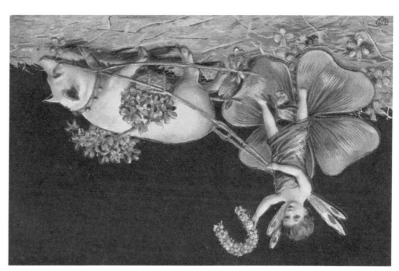

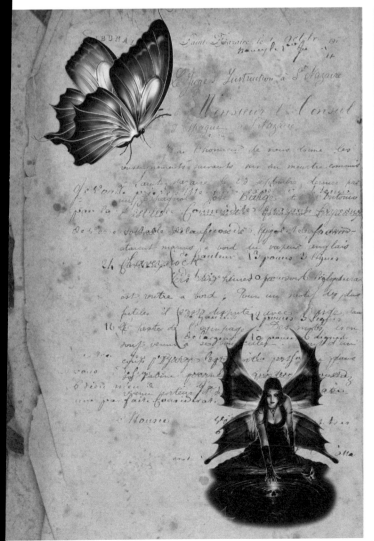

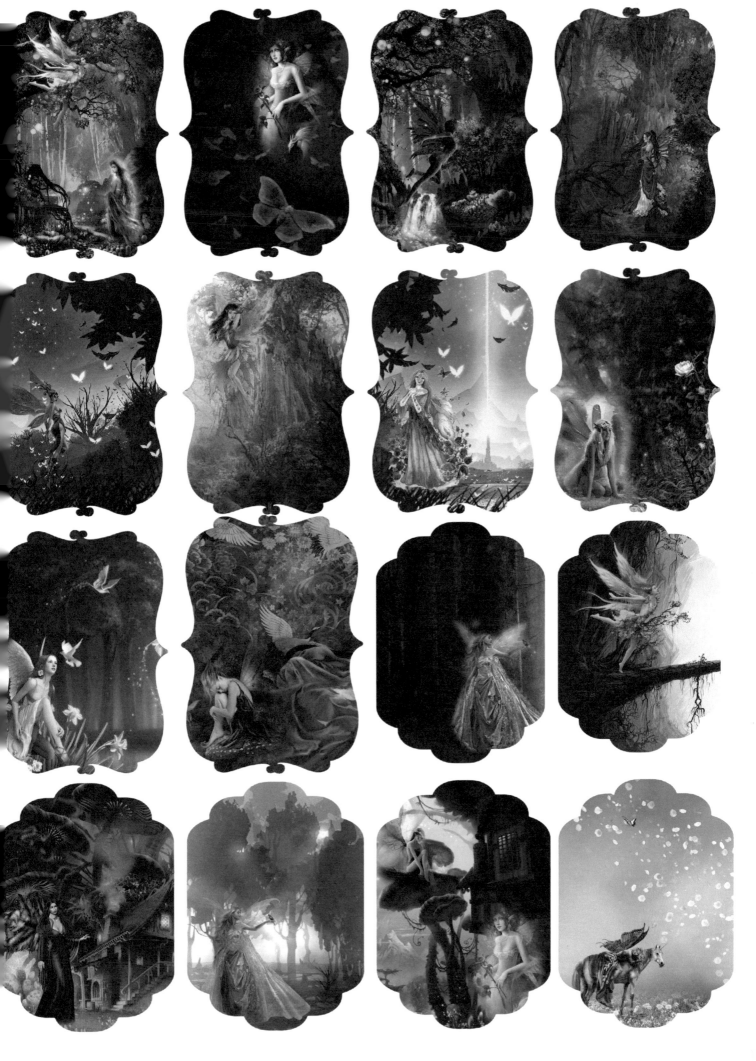

lous

would be e

the best cont

Second from

chairman Founda

There is no

see why this

beg to say th

tation In und

work was

a matter o

but or en

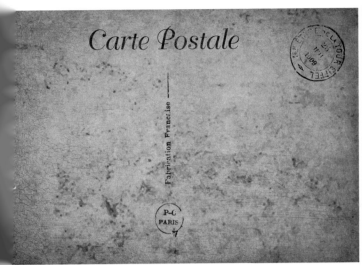

Dream of fairies like when you were a child

Fairies can't be seen Unless you believe in them.

Made in United States
Troutdale, OR
11/26/2023

14969632R00033